Mystic Musings

CARLTON J. BULLER

The Rhyme and Reason

of

Interesting Insights

in

Lots of Good Stories

Copyright © 2010 Carlton J. Buller
All rights reserved,
Including the right of reproduction
In whole or in part in any form whatsoever

Published by FairWeather Publications
Cover concept by Carlton J. Buller
Cover design by Andrea Dillon
Interior concept by Carlton J. Buller
Interior layout by BookSurge
Edited by Carlton J. Buller

Library of Congress Control Number: 2009906794

Buller, Carlton J.
Mystic Musings/Carlton J. Buller

ISBN: 978-0-9701238-1-7

Manufactured in the United States of America

Visit www.booksurge.com to order additional copies.

Acknowledgment

If we are born into a family according to lessons needed,
Some to be taught, others heeded,
What does mine say about giving and receiving,
love and forgiveness,
Understanding and kindness,
And the extent to which my trust
Is robust?

How about patience, leadership and humility,
Even empathizing ability?
Are there points to earn
For painful lessons we learn?
And what about respect and gratitude,
and laughing and crying,
Even getting old and dying?

    I wish to express my sincere gratitude and appreciation to my Mom and Dad, my sisters, Therese, Althea and her husband Mark and daughter Jeane', my brother Gilroy and especially my sister Phyllis, and brother Kelsie Jr. and his wife Tina.

    Thanks for all the lessons I have received and the opportunities to give a little in return. May you all find the peace, prosperity and happiness you so richly deserve.

This book is dedicated to seekers who travel far and wide, only to find the long and winding road leading right back inside themselves, where they eventually discover that elusive something they have always been seeking.

Foreword

While this book is filled with rhythm and rhyme of myriad metered verses, it is far more than just a collection of poems assembled into a book of poetry. Some very serious topics are explored. But light humor, liberally sprinkled throughout, adds an entertaining quality to the unique treatment of unconventional material that is also spiritual in many ways.

The author's intent is to be thought provoking, entertaining and spiritually uplifting. The pace is quick and varied, and the flow is designed so that you turn the very last page with a smile in your heart. And by the time you close the back cover, that smile will have enveloped your entire being.

Happy musing!

Contents

FOREWORD

I. APPETEASERS 3

1. Stillness 5
2. Spiritual Nourishment 7
3. Meaning and Purpose 9
4. Guidance 11
5. Fog City 13
6. Twilight 15
7. The Touch 17
8. Eyes 19
9. Mesmerized 21

II. LOW CALORIE 23

1. Moonshine 25
2. Sunset 27
3. The Beach 29
4. Grist 33
5. Reverie 35
6. Frigate 37
7. Flight 39

III. FOOD FOR THOUGHT ... 41

1. Choices ... 43
2. Wondering ... 45
3. State of Knowing ... 49
4. Lessons ... 51
5. Truth ... 53
6. The Present ... 57
7. Blessings ... 59
8. Cosmic Flight ... 61
9. Creative Insights ... 63
10. The Creative Principle ... 65
11. Ultimate Success ... 67
12. Overnight Success ... 69
13. Masterpiece ... 71

IV. SOUL FOOD ... 73

1. For You ... 75
2. Brothers ... 77
3. Enlightenment ... 79
4. Quiet Storm ... 81
5. Spirits ... 83
6. Mortality ... 85
7. Transcendence ... 87
8. Conceive and Believe ... 91
9. Creation ... 93
10. Insight ... 95
11. Wisdom ... 99
12. Experience ... 101
13. Traveler ... 103
14. Reflections ... 107

V. SWEET AND SPICY 109

1. Pretty Woman 111
2. Cozy Corner 113
3. Rose 115
4. Sweet Melody 117
5. Sweet Memory 119
6. The Hunt 121
7. Surprise 123
8. Spellbound 125
9. Jealousy 127
10. Emotion 129

VI. DESERT 131

1. Sweetness 133
2. Brown Sugar 135
3. Bun 137
4. Fruit 139
5. Bread 141

VII. HEARTBURN 143

1. Crisis 145
2. Illusion 147
3. Legacy 149
4. Puppet Master 151
5. Pain 153
6. Walls 155
7. War 159
8. Insanity 161
9. Why 163

VIII. TRANSITIONS — 165

1. Patriarch — 167
2. Careless Words — 169
3. Speak Kindly — 171
4. Fall — 173
5. Reality — 175
6. Conan — 177
7. Cycle of Life — 181

IX. HAIKU — 183

1. Seaside — 185
2. Naturally — 187
3. Elemental — 189
4. Musical — 191
5. Predatory — 193

X. PLAYFULLY SERIOUS — 195

1. Contemplation — 197
2. Morning Show — 199
3. The Room — 201
4. Rainforest — 203
5. Visualization — 207
6. Dream — 219

XI. SERIOUSLY PLAYFUL — 225

1. Good Day — 227

Mystic Musings

1.
Appeteasers

Stillness

Fear not that I blunder
When seemingly alone I ponder.
Worry not for me
If a recluse I appear to be.
And if congested roads I do not travel,
It is not that my life is soon to unravel,
Or even that I am somber and morose.

Instead, enthralled by whispers of wondrous prose
And music and song in silent verse,
I marvel at the absolute brilliance of the universe
In concealing the wisdom of the ages
Deep within the serene pages
Of nothingness
And stillness.

Spiritual Nourishment

Way up high and far away,
Exactly where I cannot say,
A silent stream braves cranny and nook,
Eventually, becoming a brook.
Before long, a waterfall
Down the mountain does fall,
Frothing noisily to the valley floor.

This brook, then suddenly brook no more,
Soon begins a gradual flow,
Not too fast and not too slow,
All the while nourishing
And nurturing,
As it meanders through the vastness
Of my unsuspecting consciousness.

Meaning and Purpose

If I my steps could go back and retrace,
Mindful of opportunities missed along the way,
I could not just my missteps seek to replace
With perfect execution of all I do and say,
But my life I could fill with affluence and success
And all the trappings of the rich and famous,
From fancy cars I could possess
To mansions truly incredulous.

My purpose though would be ill served,
And my existence perhaps not nearly so fulfilling.
For if one really wants what is deserved,
A few challenges in life can be so revealing.
Better instead to find meaning and purpose
In whatever circumstance eventually befalls us.

Guidance

Mysteriously again it materialized,
More like an awareness inside, deep down.
As always, unable to be categorized,
This time vivid, more shape than sound.

Other times, occasionally whispering
Wisdom and guidance 'twas there to deliver.
Then less feeling more like hearing
A crystal clear meandering river

Rambling round the solar plexus,
Not much lower sometimes higher,
Always between the gut and hypothalamus,
Disappearing again into thin ether.

Fog City

The thick, grey, billowing mass
Marauded across
The peninsula
Blanketing everything like a giant medusa,
Forcibly separating earth from sunny sky,
Taking prisoner all but the most high.

Then, as if suddenly a change of heart it suffered,
Silently, it withdrew from all it had buffered.
And the sun no longer vanquished,
It's temporarily relinquished
Aura of invincibility it did regain,
And the earth was able to breathe again.

Twilight

Crystal clear blue
Gradually fades to gray.
Bidding adieu,
Waves cease to break and spray.

Precocious pigeons retire to shadowy eaves;
No safer place is there to stay.
Once rhythmically fluttering leaves
Can only gently sway.

On land and darkening sea
Daylight slowly surrenders to decay.
Reminiscent of a Christmas tree,
Twinkling lights now punctuate the bay,

As orange hues
Grow dim and melt away,
And nightingales soulfully sing the blues
To mourn the passing day.

APPETEASERS

The Touch

Persistent yearnings for elusive dreams,
Questing born of deep conviction,
Conflicted passions, silent screams,
Patterns characteristic of deep addiction.

Physical journeys to places not yet showing,
Solitary roads to internally travel,
Imaginary beacons all silently glowing,
Ensuring it doesn't unravel.

Fraught with danger this frontier trail,
Specifically, doubt and fear.
Naturally designed to try to make you fail,
They're like whispers in your ear.

You tell yourself you'll succeed or die trying.
You love what you're doing so much
You're not afraid of dying.
Then, you discover you have the Midas touch.

Eyes

Oftentimes, like two way mirrors,
    They act as a porthole
    For viewing what occurs
    Deep inside my soul.

Other times, they're not so clear,
    Whether dry
    Or shedding a tear
    From emotions gone awry.

Through open eyes I look,
Closing them when I want to see,
Or hear the sound of a babbling brook
    Running wild and free.

For that is when the third one opens,
    Unlocking perceptive ability.
Much the same as a telephoto lens,
    Enhancing clairvoyant acuity.

Mesmerized

At the end of the quay in the middle of the bay,
Completely mesmerized by the gentle sway,
Watching cargo and passengers trading places
In and out of cramped spaces,
I fantasized about one day becoming a man
And traveling to some wonderful, faraway land.

Then suddenly, as if fantasy now reality,
The entire dock and me
Began to dance about as we slowly departed.
But to my dismay, while we indeed had parted,
I remained riveted to the plank on the quay,
While the boat and my dream both faded away.

2.
Low Calorie

LOW CALORIE

Moonshine

We sat and watched, my siblings and me,
Way back when we had no TV,
And the town was small,
And four floors were considered tall.

And instead of frightening
The thick dark blanket was so inviting,
As night enveloped day
And twinkling lights came out to play,

Like a trillion chickens covering the earth,
Carefully watched over, as they pecked at dirt,
By an ever vigilant, patient mother hen,
Who even way back then

Seemingly our actions misconstrued,
Concluding we were part of her brood,
Laying out a magic carpet
To protect us from getting wet,

As we traversed the golden highway
That shimmered all the way to the end of the bay,
Lighting the way
Almost as bright as day,

So we could easily and safely follow
The reflection of her halo,
As she silently beckoned for all to see,
All the while entertaining my siblings and me.

Sunset

As the bright orange sun wearily
Gasps its final breath and seemingly
Slips beneath the now gray,
Somber waters at the end of the expansive bay,

And the eerie march of dark, menacing
Shadows continues unabated, the once advancing
Daylight now in full retreat,
Two lovebirds instinctively shift in their seat,

Adjusting insufficiently protective attire,
Thinking gleefully of a warm, cozy fire,
Remaining outside, snuggling closer, determined the final act to catch.

They watch
As this magnificent orange furnace puts up its fiercest fight,
Then finally, surrenders to the night.

LOW CALORIE

The Beach

I grew up practically on the beach,
Where on hot summer days we sought relief.
Protected by the barrier reef,
'Twas a very beautiful Belizean beach.

Moved to Los Angeles close to the beach;
Very rarely went near.
But the few times I did get there,
The water was way too cold at the beach.

Then I lived overseas by the beach.
This one not very typical,
Unlike Los Angeles, warm and tropical.
Very inviting this Guamanian beach.

From Santa Cruz to Stinson Beach,
Monterrey to Bodega Bay,
Wonderful to stand and watch the spray,
As waves crash the rocks near the beach.

Charming ambience at this type of beach.
Sparsely populated like most
Sprawled along the northern California coast,
Typified by the remote, hard to reach beach.

Part of the attraction hiking down to the beach.
Never any intrusion
Due to the relative seclusion.
Perfect spot to have a nude beach.

But my fondness for this type of beach
More because of the pristine
And serene
And mesmerizing quality of the beach,

Like frothing surf roaring loudly at the beach,
Driven by the incredible power of the Pacific,
And driftwood, all weather beaten and artistic,
Holding silent testimony at the beach.

And much more freedom at the isolated beach,
And here and there the occasional couple
Privately appreciating the paucity of people,
And campfires at night romanticizing the beach.

But despite the charm of this type of beach,
When in need of some serious relaxation
I close my eyes and find a location
Somewhere on a Belizean beach.

LOW CALORIE

Grist

A farmer heads home with his mule and cart,
Loaded with produce and a big, round stump.
The mule was old and thin as a dart,
The stump smooth, except for a bump.

An artist sitting by the road,
Perhaps his masterpiece this could be.
Now alert, he positively glowed,
A piece of art all he could see.

Dreaming of making his stump a stool,
The farmer, tired after a very long day,
Gently coaxes along the mule,
Whose only thought some nice dry hay.

Suddenly approaching, driving like a fool,
A bright red flash, a speeding bullet,
Startling everyone, especially the mule,
Who suddenly flees like a frightened pullet.

Off the cart the stump goes flying;
Even the bump couldn't keep it from rolling.
Split in two in the road it's now lying;
Shaking his fist the farmer glowering.

In the distance a vanishing dream
For both the farmer and the artist.
No masterpieces it would seem,
But for the poet certainly grist.

LOW CALORIE

Reverie

As his chest is pumping
From the ear popping, loud thumping
Music and song, and all around an ocean
Of bodies refusing to concede him the slightest motion,
Not a solitary sound is he able to hear,
Save one exception loud and clear,
The tintinnabulation of the bell ringing in his ear.

And even as he shrinks down low as he dare,
Trying to be inconspicuous in the very last chair
Of the varnished, mahogany desks arranged in rows,
In each classroom of the freshly painted bungalows,
Just the other side of the sprawling green
That lay between them and the crystal clear Caribbean,
And clearly hears
The teacher's voice in his ears,
And relives the almost paralyzing fear
Of having to answer loud and clear,
Happy is he to finally hear
The tintinnabulation of the bell ringing in his ear.

And they run out the classroom onto the gigantic grassy glade,
Where during recess they normally played,
In stiff, creased, khaki shorts and shirts all bright,
With female counterparts smartly clad in red and white.
And soothing the rough edges
Of the tropical heat, soft subtle breezes.
But as he finally relaxes in the aromatic air,
All too soon recess and reverie both disappear,
As the tintinnabulation of the bell rings loudly in his ear.

LOW CALORIE

Frigate

With apparent ease that does belie
Power and speed and an eagle eye,
Surfing majestically on currents and gusts,
Her speed and direction she adjusts,

By imperceptible twist of feather
And forked tail, moving together
With absolute precision
And economy of motion.

Then, back dropped by clear blue skies
She spies,
Patiently waiting,
All the while calculating

The most precise instant at which
To twitch
Her muscles and fold
Her wings and plummet in controlled
Free-fall
To an appointment with her precious haul.

LOW CALORIE

Flight

A running start, a quick take off,
Gradual ascension to freedom aloft.
Soaring effortlessly on featherless wings,
Relishing all the happiness it brings.

Feels perfectly natural this ability to fly,
Becoming almost one with the sky.
Idly soaring over meadows and moors,
Even as darkness obscures.

Never ever sufficient to prevent,
Absence of light actually triggers the event.
When I lay down is when I rise,
Having barely had time to close my eyes.

I take my place in the friendly skies,
Totally free from all earthly ties.
So very real it seems to me,
This flight of fantasy in my dream I see.

3.
Food for Thought

Choices

I think about the life I might have had
Had I made choices that weren't half bad.
Perhaps a wife and children of my own,
Possibly by now all grown,

And all the accoutrements of success,
Including material things I could possess.
But I might not have been the same lad,
Maybe not even had the same choices I had,

Had I ignored alternatives presented
And chosen the path more frequented.
For different choices surely
Would have been made purely

In the context of the particular set
Of circumstances. And it's almost a sure bet
That different choices
Would also have altered those circumstances.

And I might have found
That I had to navigate around
A whole new set of challenges,
Designed to bring about the changes

Necessary to fulfill
The purpose of my existence and will
Of the universe,
Which through this lifetime I currently traverse.

FOOD FOR THOUGHT

Wondering

How does one even begin to get the vaguest of notions
that there is such a thing as finding oneself?

How is it possible to know for oneself, if one becomes
convinced to search for the self, why it is important
to try to find oneself?

How would one know how to find himself, if he becomes
convinced he really needs to search for himself?

How could one possibly find himself, after becoming
aware he should be searching for himself, if he has
to search all by himself?

How does one ever find himself, when he doesn't
even know where he should begin to look, if he really
wants to find himself?

How does one even begin to fathom the awesome reality that being alive isn't all that there is and in order to find out who he is he needs to be able to find himself?

What about all the other billions of people, who go about life apparently contented? Does any of them know who he or she is and will any of them be able to find themselves?

Why do some get this nagging feeling that there's more to life and there's something missing and they had better find out what it is right now?

Why do others always try to find out, even seeking advice from those who should know, yet they just cannot figure out exactly how?

Why does one hurt from the inside out and still not have a clue what it's all about, but it feels so much like missing a twin?

Why is it that this strange sort of hurt, not really hurt but emptiness, is the unseen enemy – a battle with whom one cannot win?

When will the day come that he can fill the void and know that it will always remain filled, and he can rest assured his search is over?

When will he begin to understand they became separated a long time ago, and it will take their combined efforts to finally recover?

What will it take for the veil to break so that he can finally see his twin has always been there and continues to try to reach out to him?

When the day arrives, will he miss feeling empty, or will he be happy to be happy ......that his cup is now finally filled to the brim?

State of Knowing

Audible vibrations
Registering on tympanums.
Sound orchestrations
Recognized by cerebrums.

Energy in form
That's easy to recognize.
Accepted as the norm,
Reality it most certainly belies.

For just as surely,
Though not widely accepted,
Information clearly
Has other means of being transmitted.

A feeling,
A sense,
Of foreboding,
Even becoming tense,

Or the hint of a smile,
Perhaps in the eyes as well,
Lasting for a while,
Coursing through each cell.

Neither arbitrary action
Nor the result of conscious thought.
Simply a conditioned reaction
To knowledge spiritually brought.

Lessons

If we're born into a family according to lessons needed,
Some to be taught, others heeded,
What does mine say about giving and receiving,
love and forgiveness,
Understanding and kindness,
And the extent to which my trust
Is robust?

How about patience, leadership and humility,
Even empathizing ability?
Are there points to earn
For painful lessons we learn?
And what about respect and gratitude, and laughing
and crying,
Even getting old and dying?

And how will I know
When I've learned enough, or that others can grow
From what I was fortunate to teach?
Will that be when a state of spiritual
enlightenment I finally reach?

If I finish early must I leave right away?
So if I'm old and gray, I hadn't finished teaching or learning and I got to stay?
And when finally I kick the bucket
Will it be because with all my heart I've learned and I've taught and there is no longer anything in it?

Truth

I'm conceived

I 'm born

I sit up

I try to stand

But for a while all I do is creep

I ask

Tell

Hear

Feel

And sometimes too I even weep

I taste

I smell

I eat

I sleep

And oftentimes I ponder deep

I study
I Work
I Dream
And play
And even try to find my way

I talk
I walk
And run
And ride
And also get to drive a jeep

I camp
And Swim
And Fish
And Hike
And then I climb a hill so steep

And looking down from atop that hill,
Wondering if I ever will,
Understanding I may never still
Find a purpose I can forever fulfill,

I continue trudging as I often do,
Through hills and valleys
And streets and alleys,
Thinking I am long overdue.

And if it cannot find me
Perhaps I will find it.
Yet still 'The Truth' I cannot see.
So I continue to sit

And stand, and run, and ride, and walk,
And study, and work, and sleep, and pray,
And taste, and smell, and ask, and tell, and talk,
And live.., and breathe…, and dream…, and play

On this never ending merry-go-round,
Until finally one day, full circle come it may.
And suddenly realizing me it has found,
What in the world on that day will I say?

The Present

It's been said that today is a gift – the present.
But it doesn't last,
Is never re-sent
And leaves me holding onto the past.

Yearning for something greater than me,
Hoping it will set me free,
I close my eyes
And fantasize
To see what I can see.

I sense I'm here for a special purpose,
Not to be glamorous,
Neither bourgeoisie.
Myself I try to hypnotize
To discern what it might be.

Numerous possibilities immediately appear,
Several vivid; others unclear,
All attractive I must agree.
I try my best to recognize
Which one holds the key.

Suddenly, I receive the greatest insight.
Simply focus on what feels right,
Whether just one or a potpourri.
Then it's time to actualize
And turn it into reality.

Make the best use of your reverie
And design a gift that keeps on giving.
Postmark it for future delivery,
Then return to the present to begin receiving.

Blessings

I awoke today and tallied the score,
Opened my eyes and added one more,
And then another when I got out of bed
And had some eggs with a slice of bread.

As the count increased each hour of the day,
It dawned on me I had to give some away.
So I started subtracting as I blessed each thing,
But it further increased instead of decreasing.

I later learned through principled living,
The very act of giving
Multiplies each blessing.
And I finally understood what I'd been missing.

It is equally important to give and receive,
But in giving to receive only yourself you deceive.
Receiving fulfills a far nobler purpose,
Allowing others the opportunity to be generous.

FOOD FOR THOUGHT

Cosmic Flight

To know without knowing,
Access streams of consciousness,
Yet fail to see what they are showing,
Perhaps we regress,

Or simply lack the ability
To uncover what we suppress,
And set ourselves free
To explore abilities we possess.

All that has happened
Is yet to occur,
Especially such that do impend,
Simply preparing to recur.

Feelings, thoughts, perhaps events,
Oftentimes do they portend.
To comprehend universal intents
Just means not if but when.

Imagine the possibilities then,
Both of recognizing and accepting
And taking action based on an omen,
With all the benefit afforded by preplanning.

Beyond anticipating events
To actually influencing the score,
Harness universal currents;
Spread wings and finally soar.

Creative Insights

Fame or fortune, wealth or lack of it,
Neither has bearing on the failure or success
Of anyone wishing to change a single habit,
Or make a difference in lives countless.

The creation of anything, material or not,
Requires dedication and singularity of purpose,
Such that one willingly sacrifices house and lot,
And with laser like focus,

Determinedly and continuously directs
All energy and attention
At the effort one expects
To bring the vision to fruition.

And if the drive and dedication are of sufficient
Magnitude to compel such extraordinary
And unwavering commitment,
One invariably encounters necessary

And unparalleled collaboration from the universe,
In the location and acquisition
Of each and every resource
Required to accomplish the mission.

The Creative Principle

Creating something is really as simple as
Believing in the innate ability one has,
And accepting the premise that it will materialize,
If one simply tries.

It matters not how large or small the project is,
Nor if one has the knowledge, skills, or abilities.
The only difference that can portend
Is how long it takes to achieve the end.

Any lacking knowledge, skill, or ability
Can be acquired in advance of the activity,
Or in parallel with project execution,
On the basis of continuing education.

So long as a person has a vision,
A burning desire to embark on a mission,
The drive and determination to sustain the effort
And the sense of immediacy to actually set forth
On the mission that has been devised,
The vision is bound to be realized.

And required resources will be presented
At appropriate and serendipitous, yet intended
Moments in the creative adventure,
As universal law steps in to support the venture,
By rewarding ingenuity
And making things as they were meant to be.

Ultimate Success

The process of success is like growing a tree
All the way from seed to maturity.
First there's the idea of what you want it to be,
Then the effort to make it reality.

The image you have is very clear.
It's exactly the tree you intend to grow.
You kick the effort into high gear,
Selecting the right seed, proceeding to sow.

Your faith in the process now really important,
Initial efforts seemingly fail to bear fruit.
While beneath the surface seed becomes plant,
Builds a foundation and puts down root.

And with absolute conviction
You continue your effort,
Not entirely unlike the addiction
Of betting on a sport.

Then one day a glimmer of hope,
As welcome a sight as any you've seen.
A firm patch on a slippery slope,
Glistening in the sun a sliver of green.

Newly encouraged you stiffen your resolve,
In your eyes a sudden gleam.
Lingering doubts quickly dissolve,
You're on the way to realizing your dream.

Beware, however, of the great temptation
To wait till the end to finally exult.
The full grown tree is merely the culmination,
Of multiple successes, just the end result.

Each day you persist is a successful day,
Every effort made a useful one.
Despite the absence of an outcome on display,
Celebrate the day when it is done.

For those little efforts consistently repeated
Are the basic steps in a process,
Which when diligently and patiently executed,
Soon translate into ultimate success.

Overnight Success

Not dreaming the biggest dreams,
But you visualize your dreams more intensely than the scariest of silent screams.

Not the best planner,
But you know what you want, and you want it more than anything else, and you approach it in a serious manner.

Not starting out with adequate resources,
But you utilize those you have to the best of your ability and somehow find additional sources.

Not the most knowledgeable,
But you research far and wide, in the process of securing the necessary information, and you become fully capable.

Not necessarily the most talented,
But you've never worked harder for anything you ever wanted.

Not even the right habits did you possess,
But you had a burning desire and never stopped trying,
diligently toiling in obscurity, and suddenly one day... you're an overnight success!

Masterpiece

The master dreamed…
Vivid, colorful dreams of what his next masterpiece could be.

And as the master dreamed…
His subject as yet unaware that it was even possible to dream,

The master worked…
Day after day, skillfully crafting his work of art into the masterpiece he knew it would be.

And as the master worked…
Even nights and weekends, putting every ounce of energy into creating his new masterpiece,

The master played…
For it is more like play than work to pursue the passion of creating one's very own masterpiece.

And the master was amazed…
As his masterpiece soon began to take on a life of its own
and help to fashion its destiny.

And as the masterpiece emerged…
It discovered that thoughts were transferred, and it too
began to sense the possibility of becoming a masterpiece.

And as the masterpiece went from seed to fruit…
No one could stop the combined forces of master and
masterpiece from visualizing and creating and literally willing the masterpiece into what they both knew it was
destined to be.

And the masterpiece became complete…
As master and masterpiece each gave life to the other, and
that combined force was impossible to defeat.

4.
Soul Food

For You

If I could
Make life good
I would for you

If I could one day
Make the rain go away
I would for you

If I could this day
Take your pain away
I would do it for you

If I could only
Make the wind blow softly
I would do it for you

If I could actually
Make the sun shine brightly
I would do it just for you

If I could recite a Psalm
And make the turbulent waters calm
I would love to do it for you

And if I could protect
And comfort you with love and light
I would gladly do it for you

For no one deserves it more than you
And I sincerely hope and pray that you
One day soon will have an easy day too

Brothers

Born in two places,
One before one after.
Different times and spaces,
Far apart; connected thereafter.

Respective roles previously defined,
No mere play this drama of life.
Destinies forever intertwined,
With happiness, laughter, stress and strife.

One becomes father
Making the other son.
Young or old which would you rather?
Clearly some prefer to say none.

Perhaps no difference in the long run.
Living, breathing the cycle of life,
Many eventually become father and son,
Lest we forget there's also man and wife.

As we get older
No matter the distance,
Drawn even closer,
There is always reassurance.

A different era, some other place,
Might we be related to a lesser degree?
Perhaps transcending both time and space,
Even having a different pedigree?

One now middle aged the other an old man,
A closer relationship between my father and me.
All part of the master plan,
Still father and son now brothers are we.

Enlightenment

Trudging along a bumpy road,
Burdened by a heavy load,
Wondering how much longer
Before I'd buckle under,

I stopped to sit
And rest a bit,
And surrendered to the temptation
To engage in contemplation.

For I could see
In the field next to me
Seeds a farmer had sown
Now full size had grown,
And him now busy harvesting
The just reward of his planting.

And presently it dawned on me
That, had he
No faith his seed would ever grow
His seed he would never sow.

So up I got
And began to trot,
In a better mood,
My faith renewed,
My burden lightened,
My mind… forever enlightened.

Quiet Storm

Silently it billows
Like soft, feathery pillows
Punctuating the clear, blue skies,
While surreptitiously it belies
The turbulent interior
Of the serene exterior
Of this always shifting,
Forever drifting,
Not so wise old
Hapless soul.

And like the clouds,
So too internal shrouds
Eventually
And temporarily
Dissipate, and a moment of calm
Does permeate the invisible, quiet storm.

Spirits

When no longer the final vestiges of alluring
warmth remain,
And the retreating daylight rampaging shadows
long have slain,
Morphing completely into the grandest, darkest,
most obscuring mass of nothingness,
And all manner of bird and beast have retired
to their respective nests,

And even the moon dare not show its
shining countenance,
Then do they begin their dance.
For it is at the most obscure moments that
they come alive,
And in the very depths of our souls that
they thrive.

Mortality

Unable to muster even one solitary step,
finally worn down
By the relentless onslaught, he slowly sank
to the ground.

Then suddenly, tracing the weather beaten furrows
Above his graying eyebrows,
A soft feathery compassionate touch.
And one could clearly see the gratitude for such

In a set of remarkably determined helpless
But not hopeless
Eyes. And sad indeed it was to also see
Reflected in them a sobering recognition of his mortality.

Transcendence

And now the storm has past
All that remains is a sense of calm
How he wishes it were the last
He should kneel and recite a Psalm

Unconsciously, he hesitates
T'would foster no good if he did so
He was going to praise God for his fate
But that's not usually his scenario

So how did he survive?
He has no right to make him wait
And why is he alive?
He must thank God before it's too late

Solemnly, he bows his head
He no longer wishes to be averse
He thanks the Lord he is not dead
He should continue to say this verse

He was never very selfish
He always believed in sharing
But one need not smoke hashish
To find oneself beyond caring

He remembers what is often said
The proof is in the pudding
He endeavors to get it out his head
He feels it is only fitting

Why lock it in his mind?
It only spoils his mood
When put between the lines
It is sure to do some good

Silently, he joins his hands in prayer
This pattern he shall reverse
By now it is perfectly clear
He must continue to say this verse

Hardly had he begun to write
When suddenly a sense of peace
He knew he'd spent his last lonely nite
He knew then the storms would cease

Unlike the calm before the storm
No sense there is of doom impending
Instead, in classic form
The heart, the soul, the mind are mending

Up in the sky the sun has risen
Ready to cleanse him in every way
With all its might the fog it has driven
Would that it shined in his life every day

Finally free from all his stress
Call the limo; cancel the hearse
He is now on the road to happiness
He shall continue to say this verse

Conceive and Believe

I walked alone; my head was bowed,
Heard my name being called out loud.
Looked around no one was there,
All alone in the middle of nowhere.

The second time I heard the voice,
Tried to ignore it; had no choice,
For still no one was there.
Then I realized there was nothing to fear.

For that voice in reality
Was in and out and all around me.
And I had rather sensed than heard,
Become aware, perhaps inferred,

This mass of energy
Vibrating at specific frequency,
Creating sound of particular wavelength,
With sufficient strength

For me to perceive or hear
Somewhere without or within each ear,
In some place capable of hearing
Or receiving or even sensing

Such. And while I never knew
Who,
Or what was trying to contact me,
I eventually concluded it might very well be

That the only reason I was being contacted
Was to make me aware that such a force existed,
So that I might properly conceive and believe
The reality of future messages I was to receive.

Creation

And then he finally realized
In those wonderful moments when he fantasized
Were to be found
Wisdom so profound.

And in the hallways of his mind,
Him no longer being cosmically blind,
Thoughts, unharnessed from the tethers
Of all physicality, literally held get togethers,
Plotting strategy for materialization
At a lower level of vibration.

And he partook of the sweet nectar, relishing
The labor of love and harvesting
The very building blocks upon which would rest, with exclusivity,
The foundation for his future success and creativity.
For it is in that inner sanctum that all things are first created,
Then sent forth to be externally duplicated.

Insight

When the seeker seeks and gets an answer he
Is trying to find,
The answer doesn't just come from somewhere deep
inside his mind.
But he or she,
Having opened a portal to some profound thing either
in or outside
Of himself, has now communicated with a force
that cannot be denied.

When an answer mysteriously comes to someone
that is seeking such,
It may not be that the seeker finds what he is
looking for so much,
As it is the case that information he receives
may actually have been
Seeking him. For previously anticipated it probably
was, by that force unseen.

When seeker and unseen force in this type of interaction collaborate,
The unseen force provides exactly what is requested and does not elaborate.
Teachers not mind readers such entities are.
Better the seeker should take responsibility by far.

Unseen forces computers are not, but they do behave in a similar way.
Exactly what is put in is what is gotten out, or so they say.
Treasure troves of information ready to be retrieved,
Available only to ones with the right combination for what is to be received.

But ignored by all conventional wisdom these very same forces,
Willingly catering to the every whim of their charges,
Their basic needs not nearly so extravagant as ours,
So often unrequited by mere mortals equipped solely with earthly powers.

And all they have ever needed or wanted is to serve.
And moreover their kindness and very selfless acts deserve
No less than what would cost us nothing and besides,
It is the very vehicle by which each unseen force provides.

And would in fact be the very thing that satisfies,
And in the end their existence justifies.
For as much as we need them they need us even more,
And so we need to seek their insight more… and more… and more.

Wisdom

When the Universe a lesson prepares to impart to some
Hapless soul,
It doesn't just send to the person's door a wise old man
with a pole.
But the teacher, having received indication that it is time
to come,
In the most inconspicuous manner then arrives.
For it is not self aggrandizement on which he or she
thrives.

When the teacher imparts a lesson to the student,
It is in a manner deemed most effective and prudent,
And typically it is by example,
And the student will likely not know he or she is getting a
sample
Of the benevolence of the Universe in action,
Without regard for short term satisfaction.

When a student in this manner receives a
lesson from the teacher,
Never the same as listening to a preacher,
Immediately not knowing he or she is being taught,
At some other point in time becoming
distraught,
Finally desperate for any solution,
He or she arrives at the incredible realization.

In the vast expanse of time and space,
It is wise to remember that all things have their time and
place,
And with all its infinite wisdom,
The Universe never creates the wrong outcome.

Experience

With the sun rising and so much to learn,
I'm ill prepared my stripes to earn.
But the lessons get taught irrespective of me,
That is what I have come to see.

Before long it becomes high noon,
And I begin to think that one day soon,
After doing all that there is to do,
I will try to learn from the universe too.

So late in the afternoon I finally focus,
And as shadows lengthen all around us,
When I should be teaching others the score,
I'm just learning what was taught before.

But the mighty universe will always be near,
Ready to teach when we're ready to hear,
All the lessons we want and more,
As long as we keep open the door.

So I listen and learn and I'm even more curious,
And the lessons keep coming fast and furious,
And suddenly one day I'm forced to admit
It's not how much I know, but what I do with it.

Traveler

Along the meandering path he travels, sometimes off
mostly on it,
Never stopping to rest a bit.
Arriving at the brook he proceeds to cross it,
Mostly on rock, sometimes off it.

On the other side he continues to travel,
Paved road often turning to gravel.
At life's wonders never ceasing to marvel,
Unaware things are beginning to unravel.

Around the globe on the farthest side,
Clearly heard not being denied,
Speaker remaining unidentified,
A voice suddenly resonating deep inside.

Out of the blue, totally unexpected,
Yet somehow completely respected.
Message immediately accepted,
Entirely new direction suggested.

Never realizing time's propensity to fly,
He momentarily questions his ability to comply,
And Messenger seemingly appears to imply,
Ok at some future time to try.

But years later, with no consistent action taken,
And time running out for the spirit to awaken,
Messenger most assuredly was feeling forsaken,
Though his firm faith not yet shaken.

Having failed to get Traveler's attention,
Time now for more direct intervention.
Messenger resorts to prevention,
In unadulterated, abject desperation.

Holding his hand his fears to allay,
From the cliff Messenger walks him away,
Skillfully teaching him how to pray,
Giving him something to remember this day.

Clearly though, in Traveler's defense,
Too deeply wounded to see this makes sense.
Yet, Messenger determined as Traveler is dense,
Having high hopes for Traveler's sixth sense,

Tries to reach him before he's totally hosed,
Or hurts himself on the rocks exposed
By old habits stubbornly reimposed,
As two life choices now steadfastly juxtaposed.

With additional years flown to the rear,
Traveler continues alone and unaware,
By strange winds, blown here and there,
Going everywhere, getting nowhere.

Messenger tries anew to get reaction,
This time Traveler takes immediate action.
But quick results only create distraction,
And the fleeting illusion of great satisfaction.

More years pass; the bottom Traveler reaches,
Suddenly, it's clear what Messenger teaches.
No longer a need for him to suffer speeches,
His way of life with wonder he impeaches.

He finally makes the awesome realization,
Everything that happened had some connection,
To a coordinated, nonrandom intervention,
With the final outcome his own determination.

Marvelous it is to finally proclaim,
Aimless wanderer no longer his name.
Emptiness, uncertainty totally out of frame,
To passion and purpose he now stakes his claim.

He had relentlessly sought the end game,
Instead he bought only pain, crying shame.
Yet the moment of truth really quite tame,

No romping and stomping, no screaming and shouting, just a sense of peace and a sobering realization, that it was time to begin a labor of love, which finally and thankfully to him now came.

Reflections

In the mirror did I see
An image of me,
Doing everything I did,
Helping cover up what I hid,

Concealing
The fact that I had no feeling,
Was living a lie,
Couldn't look myself in the eye,

And played the blame game,
Consumed with guilt and shame,
Fearing anyone who looked inside
Would see the ugly truth I tried to hide.

In the mirror I saw an optical illusion,
Merely a reflection,
Though bona fide,
Of what I was on the outside.

But it only belied
What did abide
In the deepest hole
Of my endlessly tormented soul,

Reminding me how teary eyed
I desperately tried
To hasten the arrival of a day
When the pain would finally go away.

Now in the mirror
The image is clearer.
No longer surreal,
It does reveal

A special place
Within that inner space,
Where it never rains
And peace forever reigns,

And sparkling eyes
That hypnotize,
Through which I see a world of beauty
And others see beauty in me.

5.
Sweet and Spicy

Pretty Woman

Feelings of pleasure
Of sweet anticipation
Like discovering new treasure
Such a sense of exhilaration

Eyes so pretty and expressive
A smile that's warm and captivating
Her demeanor playful, suggestive
Just thinking of her has him salivating

Infinite excitement as their hearts unite
Truly, must be a blessing from above
Silently, their spirits recite
Unspoken promises of a never ending love

Two beautiful souls
Pierced by one arrow
They think not of goals
Only the promise of sweet tomorrow

Cozy Corner

Silver smoke strands spiraled
aimlessly upward,
Reluctantly released
From the mesmerizing, mostly orange
Flickering flame,
Sending secretive, shifting shadows
Delicately dancing
To sweet, silky strains
Blending seamlessly with sultry sounds
Emanating from the cozy corner.

Rose

There is no debate
One poetry one prose
So tender, so delicate
Like woman like rose

Sweet and pleasant
To the eye and the nose
Can be thorny and unpleasant
Both woman and rose

So much in common
They inspire one to compose
No rose is woman
But woman is rose

Always a pleasure whenever he savors
And absolutely perfect for his repose
Sensually appealing appearance and odors
Of woman and rose

Sweet Melody

As she crooned sweetly
And soulfully,
He, the consummate connoisseur,
Expertly and exquisitely accompanied her
With deep, rich, silky melody
That enveloped them in this magical rhapsody
Which, like a miniature cyclone,
Boldly emanated from his big, shiny baritone.

Sweet Memory

Sweet is the memory but oh so fleeting,
Of a chance meeting
In the sparsely populated bay
On that warm and sultry day,
When unexpectedly our innocent, wandering
bodies and eyes,
Suggestive of feelings that did arise,
Whispered softly and sweetly
The promise of untold pleasures discreetly
Indulged in wild and reckless abandon,
Or moments not nearly so wanton.

For though inflamed passion
My imagination then as now did immediately fashion,
Cold water in my veins
So swiftly injected with a tug of the reins,
As the tightening grip on my hand
Did gently demand
That I needed to remember
That legally and emotionally I was committed to her.

The Hunt

As rivers of excitement his entire consciousness pervaded,
And down through his aura intensifying luminescence cascaded,
Deep inside a slight hint of discord and a momentary pause.
But, unable to discern its cause
He continued the chase, after his motives he did confront.
For he had no way of knowing it was merely the excitement of the hunt.

And the next time the exciting sensations took him to the brink,
He again could not help but drink,
Despite feelings of doubt persistently coming to the front.
For he continued to be compelled by the excitement of the hunt.

Then after a successful conquest,
And supposedly now having the best,
And being content for a bit, he again felt the need to beguile.
And unable to help himself, after a while
Found himself having to pull a stunt.
For he still could not resist the excitement of the hunt.

Finally one day, being a true and wise friend,
And hopeful the deception would soon end,
And sensing the need to make her case
About why he always succumbed to the urge to chase,
She explained to him in a manner most blunt.
Like a child at Easter, he simply was enamored with the excitement of the hunt.

Surprise

The first time was a complete surprise,
As he, prone with barely opened eyes,
Surrounded by seeming billows
Of soft, cozy, inviting pillows

Slowly drifted in and out of consciousness.
And she a little timid, nonetheless
Uninvited, crawled onto his gently heaving chest to begin
what was to become their nightly dance.

And routinely thereafter, this dance not quite romance,
Played out in seclusion
In the master bedroom of his two storied house in this
quiet subdivision.

Spellbound

And as their roles became increasingly better defined,
With destinies seemingly forever intertwined,
Their unusual dance now even more intricately choreographed, she massaged his chest with a rhythm
that seemed to exactly simulate
His heartbeat, and perhaps not at all designed to stimulate,

Nevertheless being so pleasurable in a holistic way,
That in that moment had she some indecorous thing
encouraged him to do he surely would obey,

As they continued to move in unison
In the master bedroom of his two storied house in this
quiet subdivision.

Jealousy

And as this magnificent dance
Continued to advance,
And the two became inseparable with increased trust,
Not even in the slightest based on lust,

And he, completely relaxed, continued to be himself,
Suddenly and silently one fateful day jealousy presented itself.

And in no uncertain terms did she let him know,
Infidelity or inattention immediately would trigger a severe blow.

But that didn't stop them from moving in unison,
In the master bedroom of his two storied house in this quiet subdivision.

Emotion

And even as they continued their nightly session
He had to make the concession,
Vividly recalling that wet, stormy night
When she suffering such a terrible fright,
Willingly came into this stranger's car without so much as a single entreaty,

This very special, green eyed Persian beauty,
Clearly accustomed to splendid household regimen, was now introducing him to the notion
Insecurity and jealousy not merely human emotion.

And they continued to move in unison,
In the master bedroom of his two storied house in this quiet subdivision.

6.
Desert

Sweetness

Warm, caring, effervescent eyes
Full, pretty, luscious Tu-lips
Contagious smiles that hypnotize
Exercise caution when encountering hips

Unpretentious, vivacious
Better enjoyed when having a la carte
Sexy, most gracious
Best item on the calorie chart

Tender, loving, all aglow
Chest of sparkling, seductive gold
Ripe, sweet, juicy mango
Visions of passion uncontrolled

A pleasure to behold
Most definitely his weakness
Even better to hold
Among other things he calls her Sweetness

Brown Sugar

A passionate kiss
Melting ice cream on the lips
Sweet aroma from the abyss
Giving motion to the hips

A momentary pause
A curious peek
At the ultimate cause
Of the sensuous mystique

Eyes again closing
As if he were dozing
Rapturous moment all encompassing
Into the bliss he now is giving

So lifelike it seems
This pleasurable feeling
But it's all in the dreams
Of the Brown Sugar he's missing

DESERT

Bun

Every time I encounter her
So sweet
So sensuous
So tempting too
Like anticipating the first bite of hot,
buttered, fresh baked bun

I salivate, when I see her
So sweet
So sensuous
So tasty too
Like a whole loaf of scrumptious, hot,
buttered, fresh baked bun

And when I am not with her
So sweet
So sensuous
So appealing too
Like remembering that last bite of hot,
buttered, fresh baked bun

I relish the smell of her
So sweet
So sensuous
So romantic too
Like imagining the sweet aroma of hot,
buttered, fresh baked bun

And I anticipate seeing her
So sweet
So sensuous
So irresistible too
Like visualizing that first bite of hot,
buttered, fresh baked bun

Fruit

Sweet be the fruit from the forbidden tree,
Not so much because it isn't free,
As by its very nature so pleasing
To all senses that prudence and reasoning
Unable to abide
Often cast aside,

While unparalleled single mindedness ensues,
And the afflicted relentlessly pursues,
Totally dismissive of all dangers to self,
None more detrimental than the fruit itself,
And absolutely consumed with passion seldom matched,
Invariably, from reality becomes detached.

Bread

Wanton desires
Guilty pleasures
Transcendent ecstasy
Like burning fires etched in the psyche

Pulse quickening
Heart palpitating
Face turning bright red
Blood rushing straight to the head

Nostrils flaring
Mouth watering
Eyes staring directly ahead
Imagining butter melting on fresh baked bread

7.
Heartburn

Crisis

Slight indiscretion
Attempts to cover
Or planned misdirection
To deceive a lover

Carefully planned
Not so well executed
The unthinkable happened
The weak link got busted

Predictable reaction
To preserve the illusion
Should've controlled his emotion
And chosen the right option

Signs were all over
It was coming to an end
Soon he would discover
He was also losing a friend

Illusion

No one knows the burden I carry
Wearing the badge of survivor courage
I walk alone; I dare not tarry
My eyes I hide lest they see my baggage

A bright smile
Some cheerful laughter
Ordinarily beguile
'Til sometime after

It's a treacherous thing
This mask that lies
It hides everything
But what's in the eyes

No one hears my soul's silent cry
Desperately trying not to end up a loser
They see someone who can almost fly
Just an illusion created by my abuser

Legacy

Trusting you is never about you
My trust in you is all about me
Unable to trust what you say or do
The overriding urge is to go and see

What if you are where you said you would be?
Better yet, what if you're not?
My folly now I see quite clearly
It was never about you being hot to trot

My ability to trust has never been vast
I live in fear; that is my motive!
I tell myself it cannot last
You'll find another more attractive

Fear soon turns to reality
I no longer find myself aghast
I've again become my worst enemy
That's the legacy of my abusive past

Puppet Master

A tug on a string, a quick step forward
A little twitch for performance mode
Reverse the motion two steps backward
Back in the box 'til the next episode

Never needing a crystal ball
She always knows just where he is
He comes to life at her beck and call
Apparently the purpose of the life that's his

Virtual captivity year after year
Never allows him to do his own thing
Applause doesn't matter; he cannot hear
Numb, lifeless, he's devoid of feeling

Having barely been made
He satisfied her whim
The ill effects not easy to fade
Puppet master now practically owns him

Pain

Slowly, silently it comes creeping in
Totally reminiscent of a thief at night
Impossible he knows it is to win
He doesn't even try to fight

Those horrible dreams, no not again
Hey, it is still daylight
Previously, the demons he had slain
Then caught a glimpse of sunlight

Now incessant, wind whipped, pouring rain
Ferocious thunder, even light
Mutant demons, a whole new strain
Suddenly, an unexpected blight

Yes, the abuses long have ceased
Even the nightmares no longer hover
But the pain still has not eased
Especially from a fight over nothing with his lover

Walls

— Not so tall that I cannot flee —
But try as I might I never seem able to reach the top,
and so a prisoner it seems I am destined to be

— Not locked up so tight that I cannot get free —
And still I cannot find the right combination, so
unfortunately a prisoner I continue to be

— Not made of brick but they might as well be —
For even as I walk it comes to me that, though free
to roam, a prisoner I must still be

— Not solid enough for anyone to see —
Yet thick enough that I cannot get through, and so
it appears a prisoner I shall forever be

— Never convicted or sentenced by a jury —
I appear to be free, but I remain locked up in a prison
that me and no one else can see

— Never even accused of a crime —
I'm supposed to be free, but reflected in eyes that look
at me the sense that I should be doing time

— Not looking to assign blame —
My plight is my own and I take full responsibility,
determined to one day change the game

— Not looking for sympathy —
Countless others share the same fate and fight the same
fight and none of them are looking for pity

— Not strong enough to keep me in —
Still not free, but I continue the good fight, which I will
never give up and someday soon I intend to win

— Not powerful enough to keep me around —
Still bogged down, but I do have wings and was meant to
fly, and I will one day get off the ground

— Not deep enough to make me drown —
The first cut is the deepest cut, and she cut me deeply,
but still not enough to give me a permanent frown

HEARTBURN

— Not so badly wounded that I cannot heal —
She continues to haunt, but she will not win and someday
soon I will heal for real

War

Roar loud thundering
Clouds ominous gathering
Raindrops steel falling

Agony searing
Light brilliantly white flashing
Innocents crying

Parts bodies flying
Unbelievable booming
Families rending

Needless suffering
Never seemingly ending
Nothing achieving

Not comprehending
Violence senseless killing
Peace never will bring

Insanity

Merciless killing
Righteous rationalizing
Terribly chilling

Life without meaning
Taken without misgiving
Not worth a shilling

Such fearful living
So terribly demeaning
Merely existing

Very damaging
This madness continuing
Nothing accomplishing

All this suffering
Never peace securing
Why aren't we learning?

Why

I want to know
Why there are so many killings in this world,
Why some lives are worth more than others,
And why we can't solve this problem,

And why there is so much poverty when so many have so much more than they can use,
And why there is capital punishment if so many believe in the sanctity of life,
And why we don't take care of the environment,
And why there are so many brutal wars and genocide!

Tell me why
We call ourselves Christians and say we believe in the bible and the Ten Commandments,
Yet we execute when it plainly says not to kill.
And how do we reconcile the belief in the right to life with the belief in capital punishment?

And why is it that this question never gets asked?
And will it ever get answered even if asked?
And so maybe it is just an exercise in futility, and perhaps in the end the real question is,
Why ask why?

8.
Transitions

Patriarch

As twilight
Surrenders peacefully to the night,
And the sweet lullaby of a quiet, unassuming,
Graceful, brightly looming
Familial apex flickers
And slowly tapers,
Sad it is to see
The end of an era coming to be.

For with sheer longevity,
And all manner of fortitude and sometimes levity
Has he become the patriarch,
And never was there a better steward of the ark.
But none stands ready to succeed,
As he becomes a dying breed.

Careless Words

In a moment of mistrust
A son did his father cuss
Couldn't keep his cool simply just
Had to make a fuss

The father being such a nice guy
Imagine his utter disgust
To hear him say the young may die
But the old must

The unfortunate product
Of selfishness and greed
Such unbecoming conduct
Over property he didn't need

One still here one six feet under
Could it be that he recalled what he said
Wonder if he ever took time to ponder
As finally he prepared for bed

Speak Kindly

Who's to say if he ever regretted,
Or even in the least bit fretted,
Over unkind words spoken in a moment of passion,
Or coldly uttered in the most callous fashion,

With precision and planning and all the cunning
Of a crocodile sunning,
Before silently gliding to the murky depths, from which it abruptly came
With smooth, swift, deadly aim,
To pounce on the unsuspecting,
With awesome aggression, perfectly choreographed and equally unforgiving.

But intent aside,
The cold words by which he did abide,
Absolutely chilling in their sad irony,
Causing unimaginable and indelible agony,
Mirrored the effect of merciless fangs tearing powerfully into the innermost sanctuary
Of the unfortunate victim's psyche.

And who's to say
Whether karmic law held sway,
Or was it purely by coincident occurrence,
As is sometimes the case with the ebb and flow of universal currents,
That his prophetic pronouncements eventually befell him,
Long outlived by his resilient victim.

Fall

In the spring of our years
When abounded hopes and fears
And pleasure from all things was derived
Nothing seemed contrived

And we merrily romped the days away
As if that way we would forever stay
And even the ordinary felt sublime
And we totally lost track of time

Then all too quickly summer came
And intrepid explorers we became
Sweeping aside all doubts and fears
Seeking and conquering new frontiers

Gradually finding our own direction
Maintaining a sense of deep affection
Forging paths increasingly divergent
Becoming spiritually more convergent

Ill prepared for the change of season
And really having no reason
To even suspect or anticipate
Upheavals it would precipitate

His sudden departure all the more shocking
Particularly in its manner and timing
I was only twenty
He was one and twenty

Reality

Suddenly
And violently
His life was ended
Epitaph now firmly appended
Perpetrator not yet apprehended
His soul and ours far from mended

Possibly
So rapidly
His soul not ready
Creating a bit of an eddy
Perhaps if he continued to be steady
He might undo what had happened already

Probably
Very likely
Why suddenly
Then one day early
In a voice heard clearly
He spoke to me and my cousin loudly

Rightfully
And respectfully
What he said definitely
Will remain held confidentially
But between you and me truthfully
It most certainly did happen, honestly!

Conan

Perhaps it was meant to be,
I may never know with certainty,
But in retrospect,
I have come to develop new respect

For the powers inherent,
Yet not very apparent,
Which far and wide traverse
Throughout this vast universe.

And far be it for me to suggest
That anyone digest,
Without further examining,
The information I am presenting.

But fact it is,
And no stranger than his
Or her favorite fable,
Told over a meal at the dinner table.

For the moment I saw him
All alive with vigor and vim,
And he saw me,
And each other's eyes we did see,

It was clear as ever
We were meant to be together.
Then soon he was free
And heading home were we.

And when we got to the massive yard,
Which immediately he was pleased to guard,
It was the perfect playground
For his size and background.

And we romped
And stomped
And laid
And played,

And he from the tree picked peach
That he could easily reach,
Crushing the seed with powerful jaws,
Along with the fruit, never using his paws.

TRANSITIONS

Then we moved to a different city,
Smaller yard such a pity,
No fruit trees,
Thankfully also no fleas.

And we continued our daily walk and run,
More important now this type of fun.
Those clearly his happiest moments,
In light of the new turn of events.

And one day as we went walking,
And the train tracks we were crossing,
Suddenly he stepped back
Away from the track,

Steadfastly refusing
To respond to my urging,
Becoming agitated,
As on the track I waited.

Seconds later a train approaching,
Off the tracks did I go scrambling,
Full of gratitude and very amazed,
His keen perception I clearly praised.

Then fate had its way
One unfortunate day,
As burdened by life I wasn't myself,
And hardly noticed he wasn't himself.

Too ill to eat I finally realized,
He silently suffered with pain in his eyes.
And as I took him to the vet,
In my heart deep regret.

For in allowing him to roam in an open field,
Never realizing the pain it would yield,
A foxtail somehow entered his ear,
And eventually his brain it began to spear.

Too young to die,
Everything we did try.
No other alternative,
My buddy unable to live.

In life we shared so much pleasure and learning,
In sickness and suffering he continued teaching.
His passing a most tragic event,
Like other teachers in my, life no accident.

Cycle of Life

I often wonder
About life and death,
Both before and after
We draw our last breath.

When a person is dying,
Is he ever aware
Where he is going
After finally leaving here?

After we have expired,
Do we ever forget
Knowledge acquired
While casting a silhouette?

Is the journey similar in any way
To coming to this sphere?
Do we begin a new solar day
With helplessness and fear?

Are we galactic travelers,
Teaching and learning,
As life continually recurs
According to each yearning?

Or is this our last chance
To literally transcend the hearse
And finally dance
Through the ever expanding universe?

9.
Haiku

… HAIKU

Seaside

The surf roars loudly
The beach takes its breath away
It barely whispers

        Crystal clear, calm sea
        Sometimes cold, very angry
        It still soothes my soul

                Quiet, calm, serene
                Unforgiving, angry seas
                Both deserve respect

        Powerful ocean
        Undulating massively
        Expresses anger

Gentle rolling waves
Softly caress the white beach
They hypnotize me

HAIKU

Naturally

White blossoms blooming
Appealing to hummingbird
Looking for nectar

Autumn winds blowing
Leaf clouds fluttering gently
Floating to the ground

The cold stream murmurs
Hurrying to the river
Flowing to the sea

Coconut tree bends
Drops its nuts in salty sea
They drift far away

Winter becomes spring
Slowly turns brown grass to green
It grows thick and lush

Elemental

Dark, brooding heavens
Belching, wet, fiery wind
Cleanses earth and sky

                Water falls in hills
              Rivers flow to open sea
                  Rise to fall again

                                Forest fire burns
                          The life cycle is complete
                                  It begins again

              The red rooster crows
           The sun knows it's time to rise
                Night gives way to day

Pink petals open
Displaying crystal dew drops
Glistening in the sun

HAIKU

Musical

=========

                    The musician blows
            And spreads his magic potion
                 Like mint tea it soothes

          The melody played
      Dancing within and without
        Soothing mind and soul

The soft notes wafted
Floating like bubbles on air
And eased the tensions

            Nylon strings trembled
       And sweet vibrations came forth
              My spirit rejoiced

                  The saxophone plays
            Warm relaxing tones flow out
                 Comforting the soul

Predatory

Submerged crocodile
Stalks with calmness and cunning
Explosively strikes

        Man takes cash from boy
        Gets in car to drive away
        Gang takes car from man

                The gray web trembles
                The fly panics and struggles
                The spider dances

        Brown snake climbs in tree
        Changes its color to green
        Stalks the little bird

Hungry cheetah sprints
Frightened gazelles run away
One is just too slow

10.
Playfully Serious

Contemplation

When at the well
The seeker shall dwell,
Of all moments most private and mundane,
And absolutely necessary lest one go insane,
And nuggets and pearls they come and go,
Even as the pulse of life does ebb and flow,
With the vessel being most receptive,
Then does come the most salient perspective.

PLAYFULLY SERIOUS

Morning Show

There was a time, when accompanied by my thoughts
alone I would go
And position myself appropriately for the morning show,
Then silently allow the pearls to come and go,
with little regard for the power they possessed.

But soon suspecting intrinsic value I hadn't previously
assessed,
I began prematurely to rush back out the door,
Trying to capture them before they were no more.

Eventually, recognizing the futility
Of this activity,
I resolved to arm myself with paper and pen,
Before proceeding to enter the den.

But I've acquired a new best friend,
Who accompanies me even to earth's end.
And now sitting on top of my lap is my laptop,
Even as I sit atop

The most appropriate vantage point for observing,
And even for capturing,
If I may,
The comings and goings of the wisdom of the day.

The Room

Sometimes standing
Often sitting
At times shaving
Never misbehaving

Mouth washing
Teeth brushing
Regularly showering
Or simply grooming

Portal opening
Visions streaming
Spirits communicating
Insight materializing

Never questioning
Simply knowing
Always providing
Exactly what I'm needing

Perfect for imagining
Or so I keep thinking
So thankful for having
This room that keeps giving

Rainforest

Craaaack, groooaan, swooooosh, kaboom!
Deep in the forest a tree hit the ground.
No one was around. Did it make a sound?

The perfect conundrum for ancient philosophers
Their time and space so different from ours

Almost forgotten, the birds, bees and flowers
Sadly, we worship steel and cement towers

Much more technology!
Far less ecology!

Craaaack, groooaan, swooooosh, kaboom!
Deep in the forest a tree hit the ground.
Was anyone there when it was downed?

Brilliantly back dropped by a sea of green
Plethora of colors like any unseen

Up in the lush canopy akin to the ocean
Trillions of leaves, incessant motion

Way down below, a mighty howl
The strong and hungry are on the prowl

Craaaack, groooaan, swooooosh, kaboom!
Deep in the forest a tree hit the ground.
Does anyone care if it made a sound?

Perfectly camouflaged, jaguar salivates
Sitting on a log, hiker contemplates

Humbled by the awesome dimension
Not even the slightest apprehension

Giving in to a protective notion
Carefully applying repellant lotion

Craaaack, groooaan, swooooosh, kaboom!
Somewhere nearby a tree hit the ground.
What if it hadn't made a sound?

PLAYFULLY SERIOUS

Too close for comfort, hiker knows
Could've been dinner, but different wind blows

Philosopher at heart, he looks for meaning
This chance encounter, oh so revealing

One life spared, dinner denied
What if falling trees are multiplied?

Craaaack, groooaan, swooooosh, kaboom!
With increasing frequency trees hit the ground.
Are we capable of understanding this sound?

Bulldozers clearing, fires burning
Loggers working, axes churning

Habitats shrinking, bellies crying
Cities growing, forests dying

Terribly alarming!
Global warming!

Craaaack, groooaan, swooooosh, kaboom!
Around the globe shrinking forests abound.
Our collective silence continues to astound!

PLAYFULLY SERIOUS

Visualization

Wispy, wandering winds carefully caressing
Warm, welcoming rays pleasantly penetrating
White, watery sand the toes tenderly titillating
Winsome, washing waves the spirit serenading

> Reverie interrupted
> Attention co-opted
> Totally unexpected
> Nonetheless heeded

Searching eyes through polarized lenses
Resisting mind puts up fences
Still relaxed, yet everything tenses
Focusing with all the senses

Each cresting wave more clearly revealing
Listlessly, dark object bobbing
Alternately showing then concealing
No, not a body, simply a log floating

Motionless solitude, curious gaze riveting
From what latitude, secretly wondering
Feeling a yearning, wishing it were me
Carefree, not worrying, casting about in the sea

Whoosh! Bang! Flash! Bright white!
Momentarily stunned, trying to get hold
Nothing in sight, just vanishing light
Suddenly wet, I'm also cold

A struggle for breath
Not ready to go yet
Presently, I see
That log is now me

Loggy Log my name
Just Loggy will do
If that is too tame
Then it's LL to you

Sense of urgency as I near the shore
Ill prepared for what life would teach
Thoughts of a new life coming to fore
Excited, weary I arrive at the beach

With loss of limb, no longer a tree
Devoid of bark that protected me
A simple log, all I have come to be
Silky and smooth for all to see

Considering the fate many logs endure
Insufficient reason to feel insecure
All I must do is make it onshore
Then aimless drifter nevermore

No nails, no screws, no drills, no frills
Neither barbed wire nor window sills
Better yet, not buried in landfills
Or even worse, filleted in sawmills

Truly blessed this Log has been
Living a life only dreamt of by men
Having grasped all there was to be seen
Time to come home to the land again

I gather myself for the run up the beach
Beginning to roll as I sense the next wave
It loses steam before I reach
I try again; I must be brave

Imagine children frolicking and gay
So too, I dance with the surf
This riveting drama no leisurely play
Just a desperate struggle for turf

Repeatedly denied, this mountain so tall
Too far I've come to give up now
Had I but one solitary limb, no trouble at all
Just a bit more time, I'll figure out how

Along the beach I drift with the tide
North to South, side to side
Gentler slopes, and still denied
Definitely not enjoying this ride

Getting desperate to break through the fog
Wondering whether it could be my fate
To remain bloated and overweight
And simply just a waterlogged log

Right on cue I hear the voices
I will! No you won't! I can! No, you can't!
As they always do, arguing about choices
Enough already; stop that foolish rant

Dissenting voices, perish the thought!
They only win battles never fought
Many mentors I call to mind
All reassure, a way I will find

But scars of abuse deeply embedded
Flashing memories of scenes I dreaded
Unable to be totally avoided
Into my mind they all now flooded

Paralyzed with doubt
I must get them out
I try to shout
No sound from my mouth

The nightmares are over
In their wake sinister forces hover
They operate deep undercover
They make it hard even to keep a lover

So aimless drifting a natural choice
Actually, more like happenstance
Perhaps a way to find a voice
And then maybe to finally dance

This dance in the surf not the one intended
What to do to make sure it's ended?
"Create in your mind the result you're desiring
Focus your thoughts; see it actually happening"

Wisdom came mainly from guys with bald head
Finally, I'm doing exactly what they said
Suddenly, dark clouds begin to form
Wasn't exactly praying for a storm

Burst of wind
Flurry of waves
Tide surges in
Loggy gets what he craves

High and dry I rest on the beach
Here I sit for all to see
All my dreams finally within reach
Exactly where I wanted to be

Almost as quickly the storm begins fading
Turbulent waters gradually receding
Not the work of a miracle maker in waiting
Simply the power of visualizing

PLAYFULLY SERIOUS

All around me logs abound
Patiently waiting to be found
Very different from the crowd
I am distinctive and I am proud

A hearty welcome from a barking dog
LL's in luck; he's headed for the log
Sniffs around as a sign of respect
Cocks his leg for full effect

Big, black and shiny, wet as can be
Never nailed; not even screwed
Salty too from all that sea
Faith in the universe freshly renewed

LL lies there just like a log
Blank canvas for Salvador Dali
Getting blessed by this huge white dog
Unceremoniously marked as new territory

Sheepishly I look around
No one makes a sound
I must be in good company
I sincerely hope they like me

Many sizes, shapes and colors
Few like me and so many others
Some weather beaten
Others partially eaten

The closest ones begin to whisper
Perfect you are, but oh so wrong
You soon will shrivel and crack like plaster
Without your skin you won't last long

Imperfect though most of us are
Sought by craftsmen from far and near
To be found soon and end up in a bar
The only hope for you we fear

About getting screwed, I am very skittish
No free lunch, they all admonish
Even diamonds are subjected to polish
Those fears you must abolish

No pain no gain, always a price
Transformation is a laborious process
If you are willing to sacrifice
You will undoubtedly achieve success

Lessons now concluded
A good time to ponder
At least I know nothing's precluded
What's in store, I truly wonder

I visualize life as campfire seating
Perhaps right here on this very same beach
But life under Uranus somehow not appealing
Better a living room of the nouveau riche

Immediately, I resolve to change my destiny
I conjure rain to wash off the wee
I will be discovered still dark and very shiny
In my mind I produce a full DVD

Raindrops falling
Dog barking
Mind searching
Nature calling

Down the beach comes Conan running
Wow! That was some weird dream
Here boy. C'mon, time to go
Weird; really weird

Hey Conan, c'mon let's go
I must! I must! Oui! Oui!
What? Where are you going?
Come back here!

Oh, all right let's have a look
Man, that's a nice log
Sure would look great in the living room
I could make a center and two end tables

Why do I feel I've been here before?
"It's déjà vu all over again"
Why does that log look so familiar?
Let's get the truck before someone else takes it

Hey, stop that!
What do you think you're doing?
Better not try that in the living room!
You're gonna get us both put out the house!

C'mon boy! C'mon!
Attaboy
There you go
Race you to the truck!

Hey!
Wait up
That's not fair
I wasn't even ready

Dream

Easy to see...
How a person could fall asleep and dream of someone in a
faraway place – happens all the time this kind of dream

Easy to understand...
How a person could fall asleep and dream of someone in
a faraway place falling over a cliff – after all it's just a dream

Not so easy to imagine...
A person falling asleep and dreaming of someone in a
distant city falling over a cliff, then finding out the next day
that it actually happened – imagine it

Difficult to believe...
That a person could fall asleep and dream of someone in a
distant city falling over a cliff at the same time that it
happened – believe it

Impossible to believe…
That the person having that dream didn't just have a dream but was traveling out of his body and actually saw it happen – he was there

Impossible to prove…
How would a person traveling out his body and interacting in an event taking place somewhere else be able to prove that he was actually there? – good question!

No one would ever believe…
That a person could fall asleep and dream of someone falling off a cliff and then read about it the next day in the paper word for word the way it actually happened – Really?

Even if they did believe that…
They couldn't accept that the dreamer confirmed the dream happened at the same time as the actual event because he went to bed just before the time the paper said it happened and got up to use the bathroom an hour later, when the paper said the rescue was completed – confirm it

So how then could they possibly believe?...
That a person actually fell asleep, traveled out of his body, witnessed a man fall off a cliff, watched the rescue operation, interacted with some entities in the dream and brought back something that would actually prove he was there – Are you crazy?

Neither am I...
But the whole purpose of the event was never about convincing anyone other than the dreamer himself that he is fully capable of this and so much more and he just needs to allow himself to accept what he already knows – he did, sort of

If you were the dreamer would you?...
See, the dreamer was torn because he accepted the reality of the event, but viewed the evidence he brought back as the discrepancy that it apparently was and left it at that – what would you have done?

So what was this discrepancy?...
Imagine going to visit a hospital in a distant city and seeing a sign at the entrance with the name that everyone recognizes, including you – That's the discrepancy?

Hold your horses...
So, the next day you see a story in the local newspaper about a hospital in the same city you visited, but you don't know it's the same hospital 'cause they use a different name — So

Now imagine this happening to the dreamer...
In his dream the name of the hospital where the rescued man is taken is San Francisco General, but the newspaper story used the name Mission Emergency because the emergency entrance is located on Mission Street and that's the name commonly used by the locals — Ok

Stick with me now...
So the dreamer decided he just had a really weird dream but, it must not have been an extraordinary dream because he didn't even get the hospital right — Uh huh

Here's the clincher...
Over the course of the next year the dreamer is increasingly troubled and eventually investigates further and is told by the newspaper that the two places are one and the same — Wow

Now do you understand?...
The one apparent discrepancy is no discrepancy at all,
but is actually the proof he needed to convince himself
that he could not simply be recalling the newspaper story
because they had used a different name which wasn't even
known to him – Yea, me too

So now do you believe?...
That a person can travel out of his body, in a dream, and
visit a faraway place, and witness an event taking place, as
it is happening in real time, and bring back proof that it
actually happened?

Um, let me get back to you on that!

11.
Seriously Playful

Good Day!

Have you ever wondered if the day
When there was no more work, simply play
Would ever come along your way
Never worrying come what may?

Never thought you would see the day
When you would work and play most of the day
And at the end of the day be happy to say
That even work did seem like play?

What if eventually you saw that day?
Would you allow nothing else to get in the way
And simply play and play all day?
Ok then, let's play!

And don't get worried and run away
It really is ok to play
And work really will always stay
Right there waiting 'till next day

So come on down to the dock of the bay
You've needed to do this in a terrible way
Put your imagination to work I say!
Sorry, I forgot that's actually play

See that ship leaving the quay
Imagine yourself on it, all old and gray
But not so tired you cannot play
It's bright and sunny and it is Sunday

Nice, warm, beautiful day
And yes, Sun does deserve to have his day
So relax and enjoy this blessed day
And let your mind drift far away

For very soon it will be Monday
Who was Mon, by the way?
Did they actually mean Moonday?
The answer to that is probably yea

And why is there a Tuesday
Probably had a lisp and couldn't say Stu's day
But I do understand having Wednesday
Had to be marriage day, yes Weddins day

SERIOUSLY PLAYFUL

See how quickly time passes away
You're already at hump day
You get over the hump is what they say
At least those having a difficult work day

Surely others must rue the day
Every week on Sunday
When they realize they must face another day
One of those that's called a weekday

But we're ahead of ourselves so right away
Let us get back to Thursday
Have heard of Thor and I have to say
Why would he have a day?

And they fry fish on what day?
The good day, that would be Friday
Then they rested on their laurels the next day
So they're right? Rest day is really Saturday?

What then about when we pray?
Saturday or Sunday?
Don't get confused from being old and gray
We should pray every day

But the game's not over I dare say
So think way back to your heyday
Was that the day you made hay?
You weren't a farmer you baked clay?

You then arranged them in a huge array?
That was way back in the day?
Before you were old? not even grey?
Aha, you built the houses where we stay

All right, let's not go too far astray
In the distance that ship is fading away
Get rid of that toupee
You're back on the quay

And there it is a very snowy day
And you're climbing up onto a sleigh
Nearing the end of a wonderful day
About to be whisked to a grand soiree

Greeted at the door of this huge chalet
By a server with a silver tray
You suddenly wonder what to say
Then all your fears she does allay

As inside the fete much like a cabaret
All manner of folk whiling the time away
Toasting to a happy, happy birthday
Bastardizing just about every cliché

And in another room just off the foyer
A more intellectual discussion on display
Easily finding the words to convey
Cheerfully contemplating the origins of day

Wondering if night came before day
Or could it have been the other way
Either way happy they say
Another birthday in the middle of the holiday

And of course they discuss Holy Day vs holiday
And how it is now just a commercial day
And all night they continue to yack away
'Till someone exclaims it's just before day

While husband ponders in an offhand way
Is day-light less of anything than midday?
And wife wonders cabernet or chardonnay
And how much longer should they stay

And as they stumble out to the driveway
Some holding on as they rock and sway
Very appreciative of the dawn of a new day
Wishing each other Happy New Year's Day

All too soon it's time to obey
The silent forces that whisk you away
When you're tempted to overstay
With this wonderfully soothing getaway

Now suddenly staring at a digital display
On the dashboard of a red Chevrolet
Parked on a deserted, quaint, old quay
At the edge of the San Francisco Bay

Having just returned with a ray
Of hope that is, from far away
Time for some café au lait
With a nice, warm serving of cheese soufflé

Okay it's been a really incredible day
But that's enough for one day
So now, in the most heartfelt way,
It's time to say

To some of you a Blessed Day

To others a Spiritual Day

The rest of you have a Wonderful Day

And to all of you a very, very Playful Day!

About the Author

In 1974 at the age of twenty-two, while serving in the US Marine Corps on the island of Guam in the South Pacific, Carlton Buller heard a whisper from somewhere deep inside. He was alone, and there was no mistaking it. It was loud and clear, and it said to him that he should become a writer, but he should not write fiction. Instead it ought to be truth – material that could help people improve their lives. He had experienced many strange occurrences in his past, but this was a first. Nevertheless, he acknowledged the message without hesitation, but simultaneously wondered how he could ever do that when he had nothing to say.

And then he went back to an existence that continued in a downward spiral, which had begun more than a decade before. Eventually, he returned stateside, where the deterioration of his life continued unabated for the next eight years, culminating in a decision to end it all one fateful night. But after driving up to Twin Peaks in San Francisco around four in the morning and parking at the edge of the cliff, he inexplicably found himself reaching into the glove compartment and pulling out a pen and a piece of paper he didn't even know were there. Over the course of the next hour, he wrote his very first poem. Then at daybreak, he came down from the mountain and drove himself home.

Undoubtedly, his hand was guided, as it is every single time he writes. But with the immediate crisis past, he again went back to business as usual, and his life continued to slowly implode. It would be another eighteen years before the next really serious crisis presented itself.

Ever since that first insight on the island of Guam he had felt the urge to write, but he just didn't have anything useful to put in a nonfiction book. Then in early 2000, after getting laid off for the second time, the universe took matters into its own hand and presented him with his latest relationship crisis. And that was the trigger that finally pushed him to write his first book. He really had no choice. The pain welling up inside for forty-four years had simply become unbearable, and the only way to heal himself was to write. Writing that first book, Stolen Innocence – The Autobiography of a Lost Soul, was the catharsis he so desperately needed to heal himself from the devastating effects of child abuse. He would later publish it in an effort to help others recognize the destructive patterns in their own lives and take action to heal themselves.

So he thought he had finally done what he had been asked to do. But he was wrong. Eight years later, he had written and published a book, but he still had not become a writer. And during those years his repeated attempts met with failure, for he still felt he had nothing to say.

Then late in 2008, the universe again intervened, and a series of events led him to try his hand at poetry. He was simply amazed at the information he was channeling and the speed with which it was coming forth. Suddenly, it all became crystal clear. He had misinterpreted the original message to mean he should be writing prose. And in 1985 when at twin peaks his hand was guided as he wrote his very first poem, he had again missed the boat and failed to see what the universe was trying to show him. But now he realized this was what he was always meant to do.

His unique task was to capture the lessons of the universe in poetic verse. It was okay to spend a certain amount of time and energy writing about nature, relationships and romance, etc. But his main focus had to be on the spiritually uplifting messages and truths that would help survivors and others heal themselves, find their purpose, accelerate their personal and professional growth and achieve their full potential.

With Mystic Musings, he has taken another step toward accomplishing what the universe has asked him to do.

SERIOUSLY PLAYFUL

Other Resources Created and Made Available by Carlton J Buller

For a detailed description of the destructive patterns that manifest in the lives of adult survivors of child abuse read
'Stolen Innocence –
The Autobiography of a Lost Soul'

To get an in depth look at lessons learned on the journey from survivor to conscious messenger read,
'Mystic Musings'

Learn how to go from surviving to thriving by reading
'Beyond Survival – Book 1'

Understand why living your purpose is the key to achieving ultimate success by reading
'Beyond Survival – Book 2'

All are available at
www.beyondsurvyval.com,
and will be coming soon to a bookstore near you

'Mystic Musings'
is also available at
www.booksurge.com

'Beyond Survival Book' 1
and
'Beyond Survival Book 2'
Are also available at
www.messengerminibooks.com

For additional information and resources designed to help survivors and others heal themselves, find their purpose, accelerate their personal and professional growth and ultimately realize their full potential go to
www.beyond-survival.com
The official website for
Beyond Survival, Inc.

Other resources will soon be available through
Beyond Survival Foundation, Inc,
which may be accessed at
www.beyondsurvivalfoundation.com

COMING SOON

Home Study Programs
Books on Tape
CD's / DVD's
Webinars
Blogs

Watch for announcements

www.ingramcontent.com/pod-product-compliance
Lightning Source LLC
Chambersburg PA
CBHW032105090426
42743CB00007B/244